now & zen

now & zen

A LIFE

Leonard Wallace Robinson

A Lynx House Book

Eastern Washington University Press

Cover design by Christine Holbert
Book design by Karen Checkoway

Library of Congress Cataloging-in-Publication Data
Robinson, Leonard Wallace, 1912-1999
Now and Zen : a life / by Leonard Wallace Robinson.
p. cm.
"A Lynx House book."
ISBN 1-59766-011-6
1. Haiku, American. I. Title.
PS3568.O3N69 2005
811'.54--dc22
                                        2005023574

Eastern Washington University Press
Cheney and Spokane, Washington

There are four seasons in the mind of man.

— John Keats

Leonard Wallace Robinson

Leonard Wallace Robinson, writer and well-loved sage, died in Missoula early on the morning of April 30, 1999, of congestive heart failure. He was 86.

Leonard was the youngest son of the eleven children born to Ellen Elizabeth Flynn Robinson and Henry Morton Robinson, a wholesale florist who served the greater Boston area. Born on November 9, 1912, Leoard grew up in Malden, Massachusetts, wandered his father's warehouses of freshcut flowers, spent summers with his family at Green Harbor on Cape Cod He was a fleet young runner and set several high school track records. As soon as he reasonably could, Leonard made a beeline for Manhattan to become a young man of letters. In the 1930s he attended the New School for Social Research and Columbia University, where he was editor of *The Columbia Review*.

He was hired as a staff writer at *The New Yorker* magazine and went on to become the managing editor in charge of fiction at *Esquire* magazine, fiction editor at *Collier's* magazine and executive editor at Holt, Rinehart publishing company. While working as an editor, he continued to write short stories. His fiction appeared in *The New Yorker* and *Harper's* magazines, among others. "The Ruin of Soul" appeared in the 1950 edition of the *O. Henry Prize Stories,* and "The Practice of an Art" was selected for *The Best American Short Stories of 1965*.

Leonard was deeply curious, his entire life, about how we locate ourselves in relation to mystery, guilt, transport and sorrow; a curiosity that propelled him into literature and, for a time, into the field of psychotherapy. In the early '50s, he took a leave from the publishing world to apprentice himself to a prominent psychiatrist as a lay practitioner. Religious by temperament, Leonard also maintained a lifelong relationship with the Roman Catholic religion of his Irish mother. (His father, of Russian Jewish descent, feigned ignorance of his large family's whereabouts when his wife marched everyone off to Mass each Sunday.) "Double Thought," one of the haikus he liked to write in recent years, was his crisp theological treatise: "Just because man needs\ God is no reason to believe\ He doesn't exist."

His New York experiences provided much of the material for The Man Who Loved Beauty, his well-received novel published by Harper & Row in 1976. The poet Robert Lax praised the novel as a seriocomic "miracle," and the novelist Erica Jong wrote that "anyone who has ever been jealous, ever been in love, ever been young, will delight in this book."

Leonard married Roseanne Smith, and they had one child, Roderick W. Robinson, of Marietta, Ga. The couple was later divorced.

In 1968 at the MacDowell Colony, an artists' retreat in New Hampshire, Leonard met a poet named Patricia Goedicke who exhibited, among other charms, an intriguingly lethal style of playing ping-pong. Within acouple of days, the two were embarked together for life.

She survives him, as do his son; his grandsons, Wiley and Grant; daughter-in-law Mary Beth; and two sisters, Mary Weidman of Glastonbury, Conn., and Eleanor Enquist of Cambridge, Mass.

During most of the 1960s, Leonard taught at Columbia University's Graduate School of Journalism, where he founded and taught the magazine article workshop. Scant hours before his death, a former colleague at the School of Journalism serendipitously telephoned him from the thirtieth reunion of the class of 1969 to relay the admiration and best wishes of the class members.

Only the rarest and best teachers of the world, public and private, share Leonard's gift for igniting in others an awareness of their finest, most interesting, selves. It was perhaps Leonard's greatest gift, and it is much of the reason so many in Missoula and elsewhere mourn his death.

Leonard was a listener, a muser, a laugher, a guide. He served as a generous and insightful mentor to many writers of fiction and nonfiction. He could recite reams of poetry by heart, even when he began to forget where he had parked the car. He won often and solidly at weekly poker games, aided only marginally by a habit of sobriety. Many of his friends called him "Padre." He lunched often with people he liked; told ribald stories; walked the conversation into deeper waters: love, literature, what it feels like to know you are old when you don't feel that way.

Leonard and Patricia moved to Missoula eighteen years ago, after living and writing for most of the 1970s in San Miguel de Allende, Mexico. She took a position as a professor of creative writing at the University of Montana. In 1984, the year Leonard turned 72, Barnwood Press published a collection of his poems, titled In The Whale. Many of his readers considered the collection his finest literary work. Dedicated to Patricia, "my beloved," the poems celebrate, among many wonders, the crystal light of Mexico, a washerwoman's beautiful mouth, a guano-stained blue fedora, odd dreams of Greece, a young runner on a wooden track in upper Maine. They end with this:

> Near Damascus
> In that mysterious event
> first hands break into feeling
> and then along the skin
> the millionyearold eyes,
> numberless, open
> like pond lilies;
> next the heart breaks into blossom
> as if into fire;
> Then last, the dayclosed flower of grief
> breaks into metaphorless flame
> and is consumed,
> leaving no slightest trace
> as if it had not been
> nor even been imagined.

—Deirdre McNamer
from the *Missoulian*, May 3, 1999

ONE

For This Relief

Six hours in loud-mouthed
sun. The shade of this maple
whispers, laughs softly.

Dazzled

Print of girl in an
apricot kimono makes
this room much too bright.

Amazing Grace

Oh, Ponderosa!
Green Prima Ballerina!
On point forever!

Perfect Shape

Exercise? My huge
spruce stands there stock still. Has, will
all its livelong life!

Suddenly

All my bones are packed
inside me like sardines safe
in their good jellies.

Ripe

Worm-heavy robins
fly in the sun, hawk-careless,
doom-eager as drunks.

Song

Were I Hindu, I'd
free that fly trapped by the screen.
I will anyhow.

A Lie For His Love Who Died At Age Twelve...

O Helen Wells in
Grade Six: nobody has taken
your place. Will, ever.

Why I Liked The Minister's Son, Fred

At twelve he called home
The Bickerage. His pa and
ma fought endlessly.

Red. Red

Three long-legged white birds
stand in the marsh. A slow
flamingo flies by.

On A Blue Bicycle

Beautiful girl bikes
by. No hands. White helmet. Oh.
Towing her baby.

His Athena

Luminous—huge—a
　　　voluminous cumulus—
　　　in-lit—numinous.

Visitors

　　At breakfast: Each fat
　　flake came down, down, came down with
　　its whole family.

Yard Magic

My high hedge turns my
pale talky neighbors passing
into a flock of geese.

Applied Science

Hawks know space-time. Knew
it long before Einstein. Use it
daily. Dine out there.

Rest/Return

Dove-beautiful sleep,
love-toned grays...Then level hills,
bring back green-dancing.

Small Conceit

Poplar branches heave,
leaves shake, helpless with laughter
at the wind's wild talk.

Turning Points

Birch in maple shade
bent sunward, went crooked till,
above shade, went straight.

Death Wish On Spruce

Met Death. A real con
artist. Makes you think he owns
something you must have.

On Elm Street, Hope

Blonde as sunlight in
her blue blouse, pants pale as fear,
strolls in freckled shade.

Salvation

Nine kinds of bloom to
welcome his dear one back from
four-day trip forever.

TWO

Salvation II

When I hear a T.V.
evangelist, I praise God
for His wild humor.

Leadership

Ike warned: "Watch the new
palship of rich and army"
and I do. I do.

Skill

The U.S. backed the
Indians' need for freedom
with reservations.

Turn About

In this classless new
society, lower class
will become upper.

Fair's Fair

The Brave deserve the
Fair and may get them if they
live long enough.

A Great Weeping

Modern art broke up
at what the Real's become and
what it could have been.

Hero Reconsidered

Stout Cortes was in
fact thin. Historians: Fat
in spirit? Stout-headed?

Tough Questions

–1–

If Number differs
from the Real, how can we
ever count on it?

– 2 –

If Language says it
differs from the Real, can we
take its word for it?

Two Notes to Self
With Conclusion

– 1 –
Write to: Max, Jean,
May, the Fields, Derek, Fred's Fruits,
Joe, Gib, Gerry, Gil.

– 2 –
Phone: Jer, Hank's Hardware,
May's Wash, Sam's Plumbing, Viv, Ag,
Gert, Bill. Give up work.

Staying Power

The imagined wrong
is always the very last
to be forgiven.

Ah Munition Makers!

Arming all to help
stop wars! Your honest concern
really kills us.

Selecting

He loved being all
alone, looking out at the
snow, rain, sun. Sometimes.

Prison

Mind knows the future
but can move only in the
now, now, now, now, now.

Mist

Why so silent. Soul?
You not speaking to me? Or
is it I to you?

Poem

Rhythm's ordered peace:
a great "Caw Caw" breaks the beat;
vowels fall like shells.

Making It

– 1 –

A bird watering
place is where a cat, mad for
robins, should hang out.

– 2 –

But he must not hang
back. Effective aggression
maketh a full cat.

Goal?

Lowering of child death-
rate by Science ensures child-
starvation later.

Take My Word

The real father of
Science? Doubt. Doubting Thomas.
Stop and think. Doubt it?

Sweeney Confessor

– 1 –

The Universe as
a provable accident?
Tell it to Sweeney.

– 2 –

"Mind" as an outcome
of "natural selection?"
Also tell Sweeney.

Small Comfort

If birds, not us, had
won this world, they'd've buried it
under guano, too.

Rebel

If you go against
the crowd because you can't keep
up, you could be right.

Advice

Sudden wish to write
old love self-exculpating
letter? Squelch at once.

Winter Guilt

My thoughts are with my
small car all alone now in
its unheated house.

Plain View

White clapboard houses
seen from the right angles, hover
on high windswept cliffs.

THREE TOUGH Q'S

Q

If form is our single
shield against Chaos, why's
it keep breaking?

Q

Civilizations
die from their great excesses;
A. Toynbee. Wall Street?

Q

Buttons were better
than zippers, horses than cars;
Better than morals?

Simplicity Itself…

Q
If the post-moderns'
esthetics are so hot, why's
their poetry so bad?

A
Because good poetry
creates a good esthetic
and not vice versa.

Safety Dancing

Twitching finch on a
thin branch; safe balancing wants
a shifty fellow.

Great Price

Angels don't hurt but
aren't free. Possible pain is
the price of freedom?

Double Thought

Just because man needs
God is no reason to believe
He doesn't exist.

Ukase

God's essence is His
secrecy, all contrary claims
notwithstanding.

Wild Thought

Could the worship of
His silence bring us all back
into the Garden?

Compounding

– 1 –

Christianity
was made for man, not man for
Christianity.

– 2 –

Same's true for Science.
Far too late now, though, to save
us from both errors.

Tip

Intelligent forms
from space will avoid earth if
they are also wise.

Early Love

Love for freedom's the
first stage of Chaos, but that's
not grasped till you're free.

THREE

The Self

She's ten years married.
Calls friend, weeping. Her lover
may be unfaithful.

50th Anniversary

He married her to
protect himself against her
beauty and it worked.

Odds

Homes Ave. was named
for his family. Went to Yale.
Turned out okay though.

Martha

Too old for ballet
she led dance to the realm of
her flat-footed real.

Heat

This philosopher
fights for his objective world
view with cold fury.

Fallen Away Priest

He watched her walk naked
across their room, thought, trembling,
"Christ" God *isn't* a myth!"

Words and Pictures

Mann's genius shines forth
ghostlike from a bad movie
of "Death in Venice."

Poet-Entrepreneur

Misunderstanding
his genius he became a
famous talk-show guru.

Stud Demasqué

– 1 –

When he loses a
hand he tells us how badly
the winner played it.

– 2 –

He'd hung in because
no real player'd *believe* the
winner was for real.

Transforming power

She adored his humble
spirit. This made him so cock-
sure she had to leave.

Envy

Ex-drunk's wife gets gay,
talky, eyes shine — on two wines.
This enrages him.

Territorial Imperative

This cool Kantian
kicked huge dents in a Freshman's
car blocking his drive.

Fatherhood

His terrible guilt
about his beautiful son
came very hard-earned.

Narcissus at 12

He knew, suddenly,
his braces couldn't, nothing
could straighten things out.

Anxious Curator

In his stomach the
gasses come and go, mumble of
Michelangelo.

Lawsuit

"Do you want love or
justice?" he'd said. "Justice," she'd
said. He got it, swift.

An Eskimo Catholic Priest

Was beloved far North
for this line: "Many are cold
but few are frozen."

Good Teacher Tells Me:

Getting the young to
like you's like shooting trout in
a barrel. Easier.

Jog for Uncles

Unless you've picked a
sure-fire gift, just recall:
Youth prefers hard cash.

Shiny Things

Every whore is
a child at heart and the same
is true vice versa.

Pour La Boue

Missing Mass is no
longer a Mortal Sin and
Jack Flynn misses both.

Overheard at
a Séance

"Laugh at Life's defeats!"
"But, Guru, That'd deprive me
of this morning pain."

Overheard in A
Cafeteria

"Daylight Saving Time
is like jet lag but without
going anywhere."

Overheard at a
Faculty Club On Jan. 15, 1991

"Yes, I want Saddam
dead. How could a dumb Deke know
so much about me?"

True Hero In Real Trench

His posturing was
awesome but his clear lack of
fear terrifying.

Obsessive-Compulsive

He strokes his new file
cards, still in their wrappings; feels
warm, sweet, safe; smiles.

The Good

Slow-witted brother
Jim's life-long paper route
paid all Ben's college fees.

FOUR

He Says

His memory at
eighty's as good as ever.
It's his heart forgets.

Endlessly

He strains to hold fast
to the too-real beauty of
the too-often seen.

Impotence

Pine trees, holy candles,
flagpoles finger the sky. No
longer his close friends.

Dodge

His lack of any
fear of death? Hoary trick to
deny it exists.

Old Tricks

We like Crosswords. Make
us think we recall what we're
only looking up.

Writer

Old, he loved seedbed
quintessences, reductions—
dust, ash—ah yes, ash.

Readying

Lunch: She spilled two cups
of soup and forgot my name.
Oh, sweetheart, it comes.

With Dirce

His soul, quiet as
a sailboat, tacks him here, there
everywhere he loves.

Daydream

Out of jealousy
Mind's become the foe of Soul.
What lovers they'd be.

Longtime Error

I'd thought "He's waiting
to die" was a cliche for
old age, until now.

Pressures/Passions

Young men quarrel, old
men go to war. Hearts harden
with one's arteries.

Beholder

A girl elephant's
body: Not as beautiful
as Helen's? To whom?

Cost of Therapy

Though insight lights the
dark emotion up, it tends
to kill all the joy.

Why Faculties
Are Fractious

To Prof. Cage the gift
of tenure led to Pride, Sloth,
Guilt, Permanent Rage.

In An Old Man's Orchard

Shrunk heads wind dance a
Masque of The Red Death; his crab
apple tree's done for.

Aged Psychotherapist

Frets: Her retired doc's
self-esteem. Phones him daily
for check up — on him.

Old Demo Pol

The Moon's been reached? That's
pure Republican P.R.
So what, if it has?

Old Poet Firebrand

His raging words have
a déjà vu feel, a real
echo to them now.

From His Nursing Home

Brother John, who once
grew them, sends me dozens of
roses he paints now.

In His Ancient Dooryard

Forsythia blooms
forsooth, yes, forsythia
yellow, yellow, yes.

Passing It On

Son, grandson believe
Science's Triumph means World's
End. Gramp did also.

Revenge, With
Time As Ally

Your walk rang rain, your
gold hair lit ceilings, you, once
faithless, now a crone.

Old Man For Dinner

Heart; just-landed trout.
Eyes; dusty blue grapes, Concord.
Mind; a soft Cheddar.

Old Wife's Maneuver

Her wild fits of nerves
are designed to get him to
get her back on track.

Old Linguist

His pee now sings to
him in a strange tongue: "Lesyl,
anjou, koon." How learn?

Old Poet

Removed all old snaps
from his study. They stirred up
feelings beyond words.

Last Love

Failure, herself, lies
down beside him, cold with her
need at five a.m.

The End